Introducing Theory of Music

by Naomi Yandell

ublished by
rinity College London Press Ltd
initycollege.com

egistered in England
ompany no. 09726123

inted in England by Caligraving Ltd

Contents

Introduction

First writing skills for musicians

If you read a book you are reading another person's thoughts. If you play music you are playing another person's **musical** thoughts. People write books and music so that they can share their ideas.

Here is a book to help you learn to read and write commonly used musical symbols. It is a little bit like a handwriting book in that it prepares you with the basics so that you can learn symbols to help you write your own music.

Using this workbook

The writing in the boxes ⬭ tells you about musical signs and symbols.

Doing the tasks

- Use a pencil with a sharp point and a fairly soft lead so that you can easily rub out what you have written if you need to.

- As with handwriting, careful to be neat and accurate because other people must be able to read what you have written.

- Read through the boxes to make sure you understand how to do the tasks and ask for help if you need it.

- The first task in a section has usually been done for you in blue to show you what to do.

- As you progress through this book try to play, sing or tap the music you write. This is a very important part of learning, and will help you 'hear' what you write in your head. This will be useful later on if you decide to take an exam when you have to work in silence.

What comes next?

When you have finished this book ask your teacher whether you may go on to Trinity's *Theory of Music Workbook Grade 1*.

Writing notes – noteheads

> **Notes** are symbols for sounds. **Noteheads** are one part of a note; they are drawn in different ways to show the length of each sound.

Copy these noteheads five times. Leave a finger space between each.

1 ⬮

Handy tip!

When you copy these noteheads you don't need to shade them.

 not

⬭ not

2 ⬭

3 ⬮

4 ⬭

5 ⬯

Look!

Notice that noteheads are oval not round.

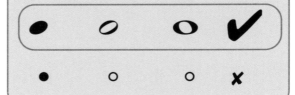

Writing notes – stems

Stems are vertical lines that connect to the noteheads.

Sometimes they point up ♩ and sometimes they point down ♩

Add stems to these noteheads.

Look!

Stems are straight and vertical.
A ruler will be helpful.

| ✔

\ or / ✗

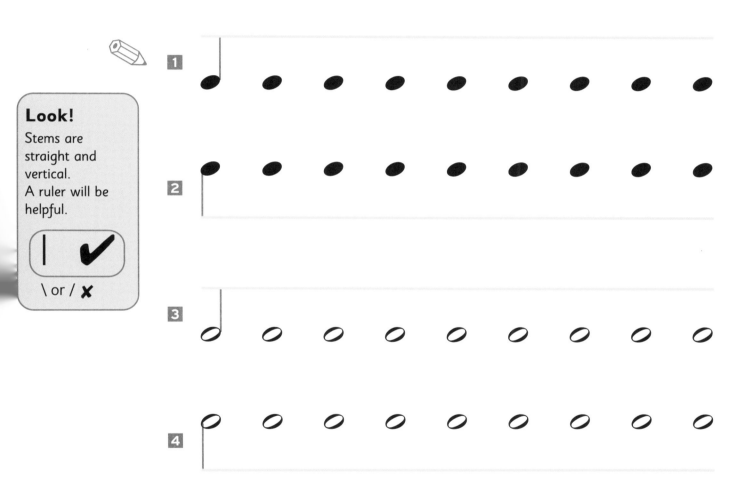

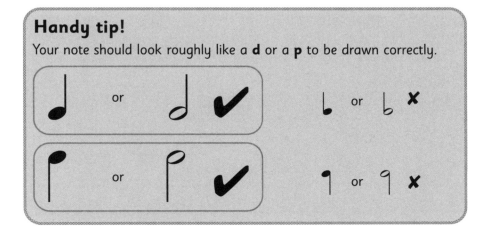

Handy tip!

Your note should look roughly like a **d** or a **p** to be drawn correctly.

Writing notes – higher and lower

Sometimes notes get higher or lower.
The length of each stem usually stays the same.

Add stems to these noteheads.

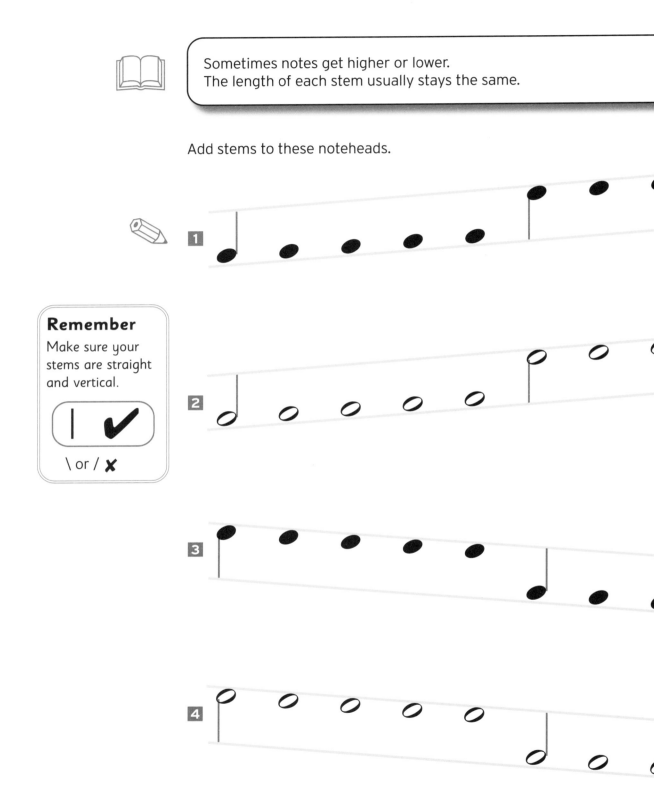

Remember

Make sure your stems are straight and vertical.

| ✔

\ or / ✗

Did you know?

In music ♩ means the same as ♩

𝅗𝅥 means the same as 𝅗𝅥

Writing crotchets

♩ = 1 crotchet beat

Copy these crotchets.

1

♩ = 1 crotchet beat

Remember

In music ♩ means the same as ♩

Copy these crotchets.

2

Handy tip!

In music if we say 'write the crotchet on the line' it means:

or ✔

not

or ✗

The line helps our eyes to follow the notes. See page 14.

Write crotchets on the line.

3

Write crotchets on the line.

4

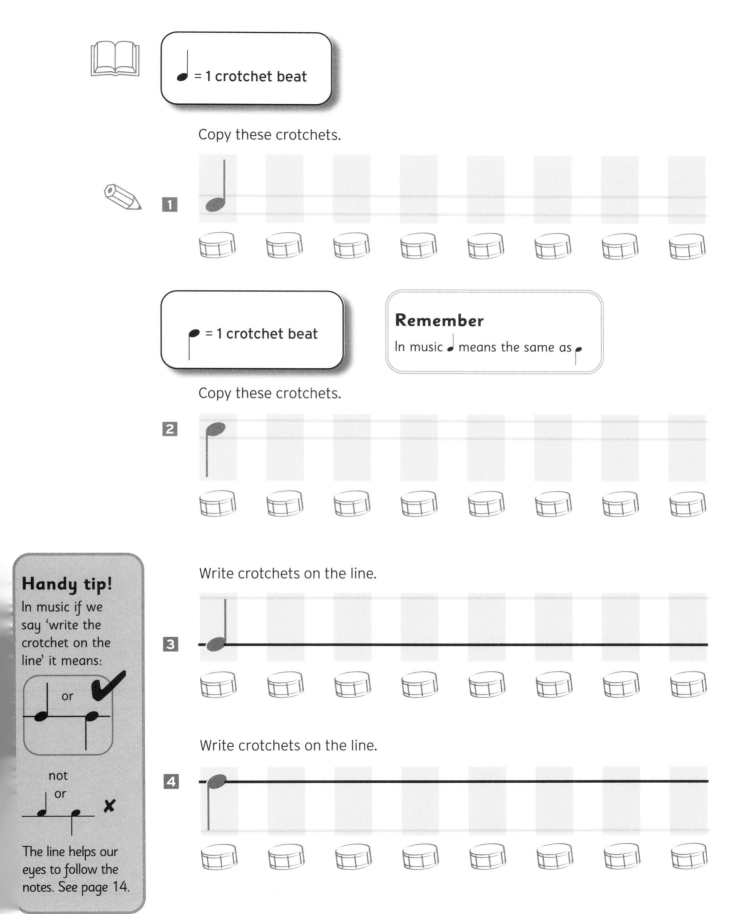

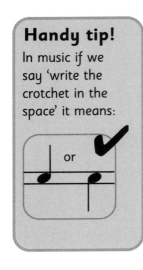

Handy tip!

In music if we say 'write the crotchet in the space' it means:

Write crotchets in the space.

5

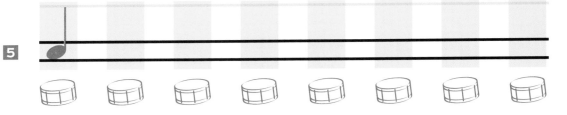

Write crotchets in the space.

6

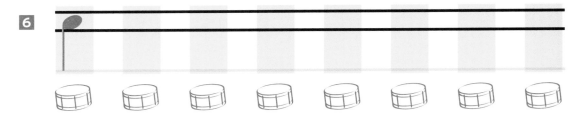

Write crotchets on the bottom line (**L**) or in the space (**S**).

7

L S S L S L S L S L

Write crotchets on the top line (**L**) or in the space (**S**).

8

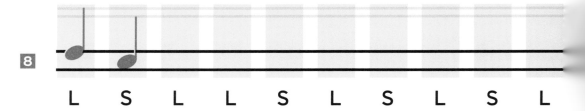

L S L L S L S L S L

Handy tip!

Top line: _____
Bottom line: _____

Writing minims

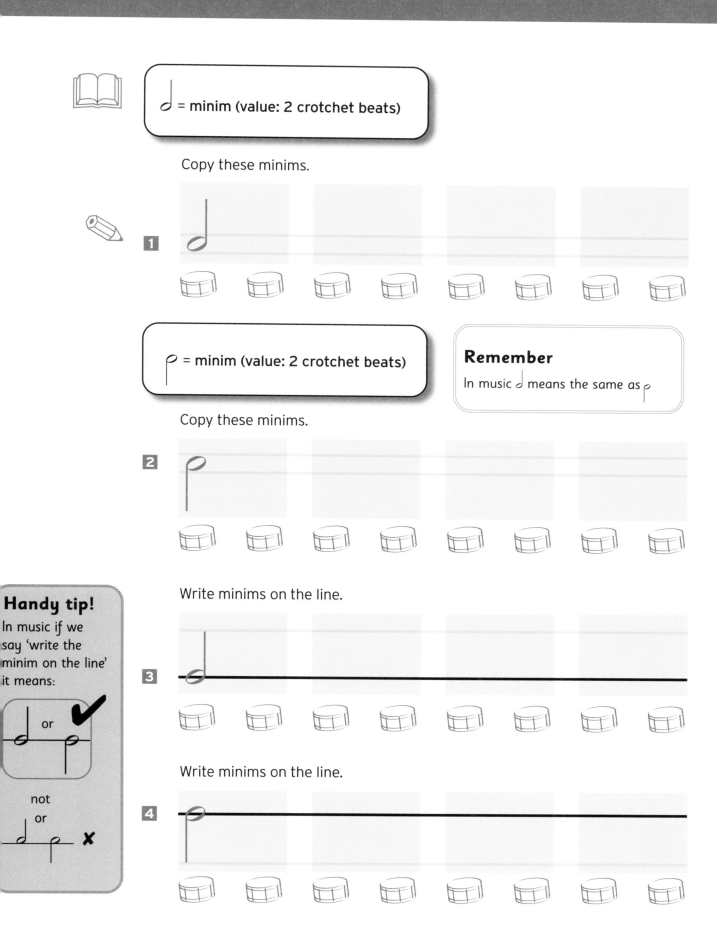

d = minim (value: 2 crotchet beats)

Copy these minims.

1

ρ = minim (value: 2 crotchet beats)

Remember

In music d means the same as ρ

Copy these minims.

2

Handy tip!

In music if we say 'write the minim on the line' it means:

or ✔

not
or
✗

Write minims on the line.

3

Write minims on the line.

4

Write minims in the space.

5

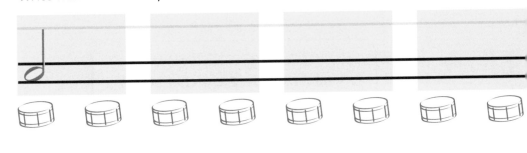

Write minims in the space.

6

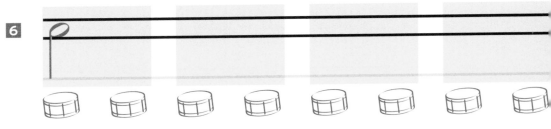

Write minims on the top line (**L**) or in the space (**S**).

7

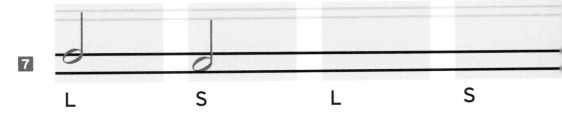

L   S   L   S

Write minims on the bottom line (**L**) or in the space (**S**).

8

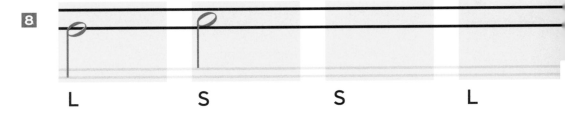

L   S   S   L

Writing semibreves

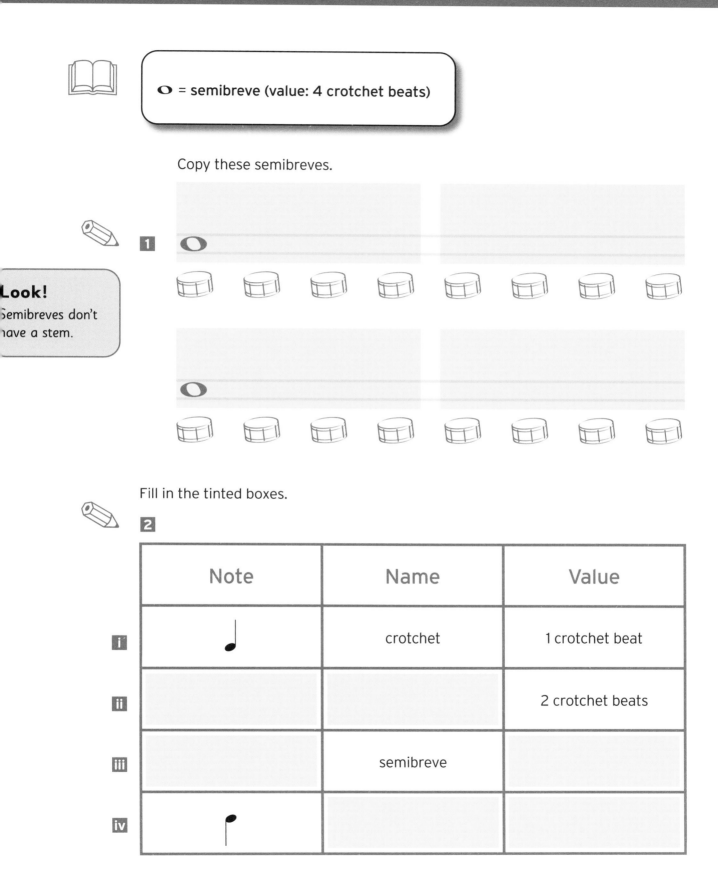

o = semibreve (value: 4 crotchet beats)

Copy these semibreves.

1

Look!
Semibreves don't have a stem.

Fill in the tinted boxes.

2

	Note	Name	Value
i	♩	crotchet	1 crotchet beat
ii			2 crotchet beats
iii		semibreve	
iv	♩		

Adding note values

Add the total number of crotchet beats in these note values. Give your answer as one note.

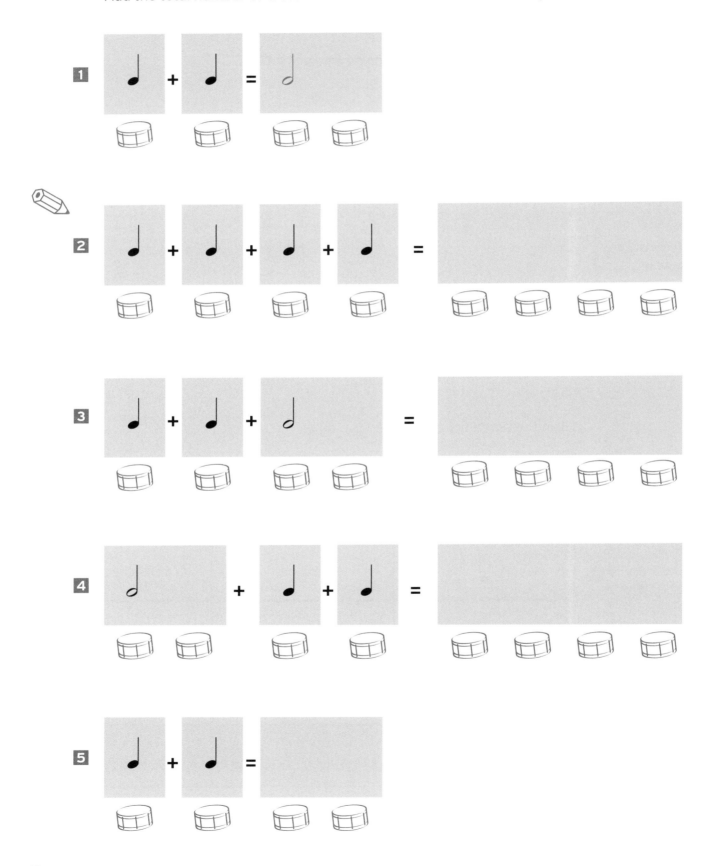

Add the total number of crotchet beats in these note values.

6 ♩ + ♩ + ♩ = 3 crotchet beats

7 ♩ + ♩ + 𝅗𝅥 = ____ crotchet beats

8 ♩ + 𝅝 = ____ crotchet beats

9 𝅝 + ♩ + ♩ = ____ crotchet beats

10 𝅗𝅥 + 𝅗𝅥 = ____ crotchet beats

11 ♩ + ♩ + 𝅗𝅥 + ♩ = ____ crotchet beats

12 𝅝 + 𝅗𝅥 = ____ crotchet beats

The stave

We usually write notes on a 5-line **stave**:

We number the lines and spaces like this:

Lines		Spaces
5		4
4		3
3		2
2		1
1		

Lines   **Spaces**

Remember

Crotchet note-heads are oval not round.

Look!

We can also refer to the lines and spaces like this:

5 — or top line
4
3
2
1 — or bottom line

4 — or top space
3
2
1 — or bottom space

1 Write a crotchet notehead on each line of the stave (lines 1-5).

2 Write a crotchet notehead in each space of the stave (spaces 1-4).

3 Write a crotchet notehead on each line and in each space of the stave.

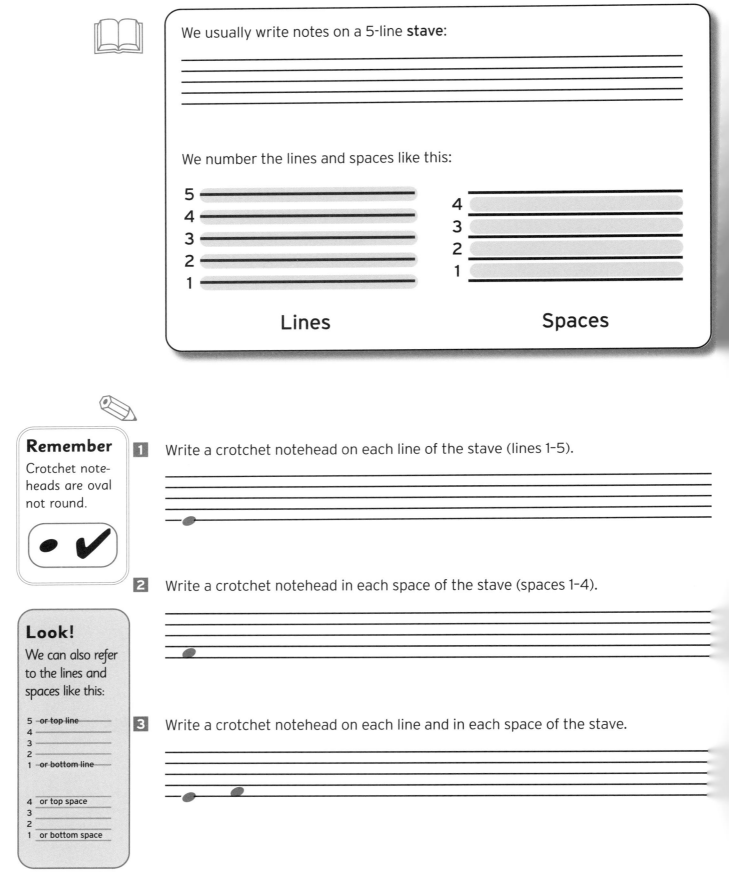

4 Write four crotchet noteheads on line 3 and four crotchet noteheads in space 4.

5 Write three crotchet noteheads in space 2 and four crotchet noteheads on line 2.

6 Write five crotchet noteheads on line 1 and three crotchet noteheads in space 3.

7 Write four crotchet noteheads in space 4 and three crotchet noteheads in space 1.

8 Write two crotchet noteheads in spaces 1, 3 and 4.

9 Write four crotchet noteheads on line 5 and three crotchet noteheads in space 2.

10 Write three crotchet noteheads on lines 1, 3 and 5.

Higher and lower sounds (♩)

We write higher sounds using notes at the top of the stave (above line 3), with their stems pointing down.

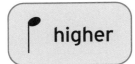

higher

We write lower sounds using notes at the bottom of the stave (below line 3), with their stems pointing up.

lower

The sound shown by the note on line 3 may be written:

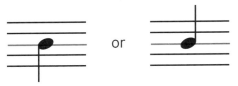

or

Remember

These notes look different but they will sound the same.

1 Write five high crotchets, then three low crotchets.

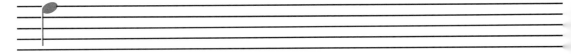

2 Write three crotchets on line 3, then four higher crotchets.

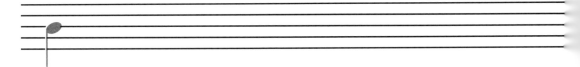

3 Add stems to the noteheads on pages 14 and 15 to make crotchets.

Higher and lower sounds (𝅗𝅥 and 𝅝)

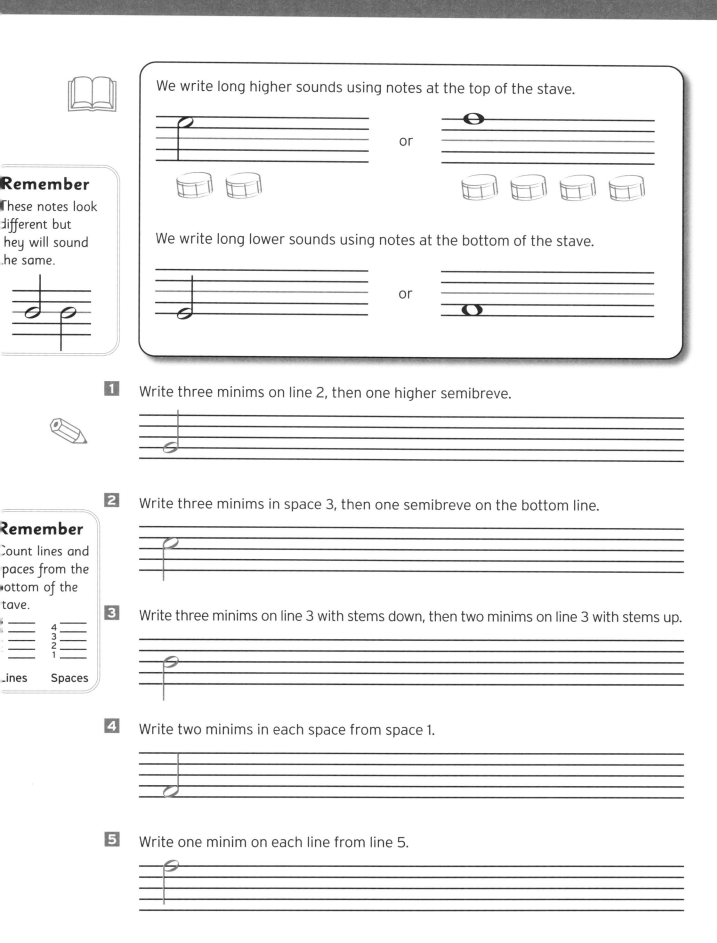

We write long higher sounds using notes at the top of the stave.

or

We write long lower sounds using notes at the bottom of the stave.

or

Remember

These notes look different but they will sound the same.

Remember

Count lines and spaces from the bottom of the stave.

5
4
3
2
1

4
3
2
1

Lines   Spaces

1 Write three minims on line 2, then one higher semibreve.

2 Write three minims in space 3, then one semibreve on the bottom line.

3 Write three minims on line 3 with stems down, then two minims on line 3 with stems up.

4 Write two minims in each space from space 1.

5 Write one minim on each line from line 5.

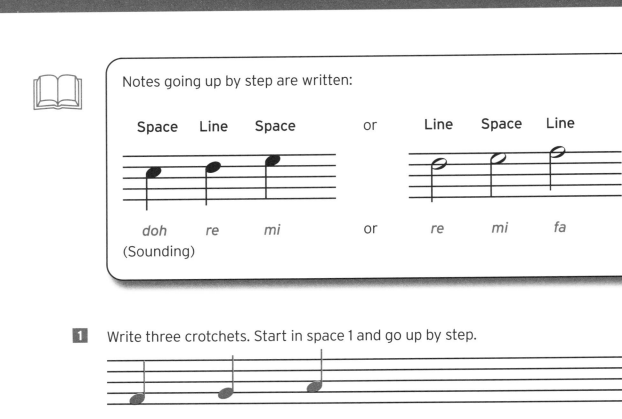

Notes going up by step are written:

Space   Line   Space   or   Line   Space   Line

doh   re   mi   or   re   mi   fa
(Sounding)

1 Write three crotchets. Start in space 1 and go up by step.

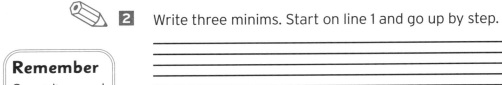

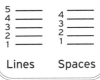

2 Write three minims. Start on line 1 and go up by step.

Remember

Count lines and spaces from the bottom of the stave.

```
5 ——        4 ——
4 ——        3 ——
3 ——        2 ——
2 ——        1 ——
1 ——
```

Lines   Spaces

3 Write three semibreves. Start in space 3 and go up by step.

4 Write three crotchets. Start on line 2 and go up by step.

5 Write three minims. Start in space 2 and go up by step.

Sounds getting lower (going down by step)

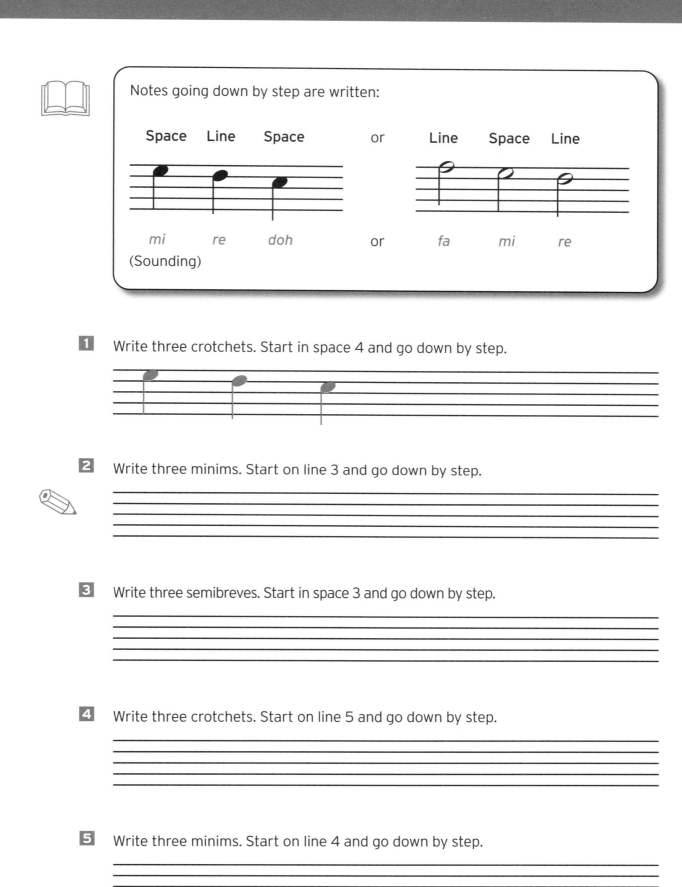

Notes going down by step are written:

| Space | Line | Space | or | Line | Space | Line |

mi   re   doh   or   fa   mi   re

(Sounding)

1 Write three crotchets. Start in space 4 and go down by step.

2 Write three minims. Start on line 3 and go down by step.

3 Write three semibreves. Start in space 3 and go down by step.

4 Write three crotchets. Start on line 5 and go down by step.

5 Write three minims. Start on line 4 and go down by step.

Sounds staying the same

Notes that sound the same are written:

in the same space   or   on the same line

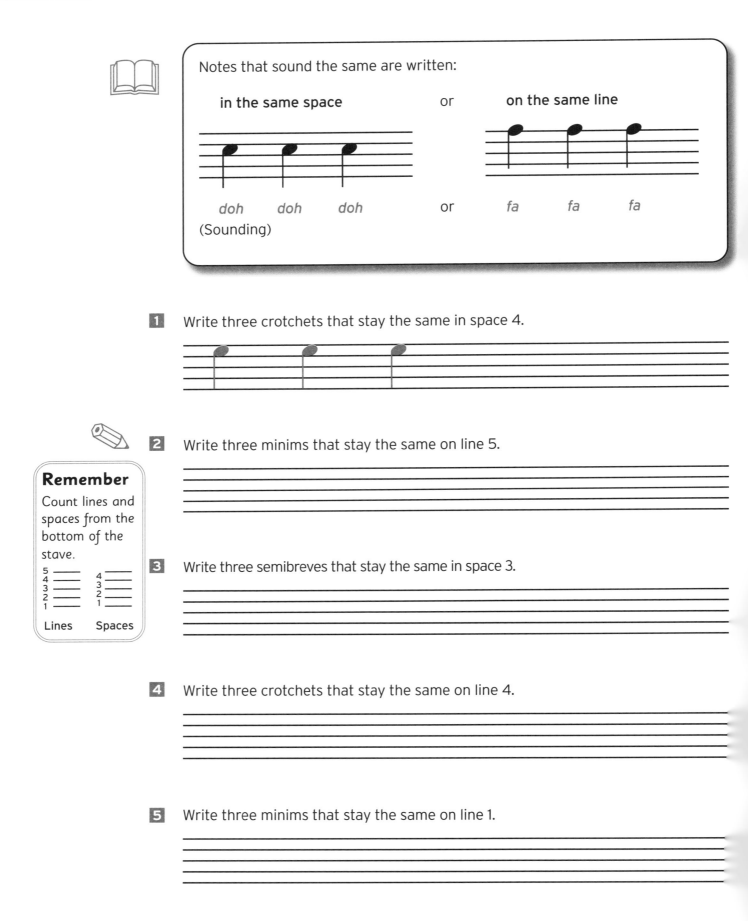

doh   doh   doh   or   fa   fa   fa

(Sounding)

1 Write three crotchets that stay the same in space 4.

Remember

Count lines and spaces from the bottom of the stave.

5 ——
4 ——
3 ——
2 ——
1 ——

Lines

4 ——
3 ——
2 ——
1 ——

Spaces

2 Write three minims that stay the same on line 5.

3 Write three semibreves that stay the same in space 3.

4 Write three crotchets that stay the same on line 4.

5 Write three minims that stay the same on line 1.

Remember

The noteheads show the shape of the sounds.
In this example the sounds get higher:

doh   re   mi
(Sounding)

1 Write three crotchets. Start on line 1 and go up by step.

2 Write three semibreves. Start in space 2 and stay the same.

3 Write three minims. Start in space 4 and go down by step.

4 Write three semibreves. Start on line 2 and go down by step.

5 Write three crotchets. Start on line 5 and stay the same.

6 Write three minims. Start in space 3 and go down by step.

7 Write three semibreves. Start on line 5 and go down by step.

8 Write three semibreves. Start in space 3 and go up by step.

9 Write three crotchets. Start on line 4 and stay the same.

10 Write three minims. Start on line 1 and go up by step.

11 Write three semibreves. Start on line 4 and go down by step.

12 Write three crotchets. Start in space 2 and go up by step.

Grouping beats (♩)

When we play music we **count**. To start with we usually count in crotchet beats. We organise these beats into groups of 2, 3 or 4.

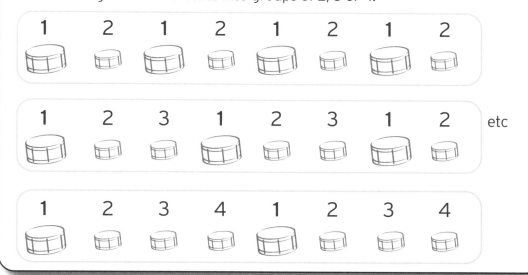

1 Circle these crotchets in groups of 2.

2 Circle these crotchets in groups of 4.

3 Circle these crotchets in groups of 3.

4 Circle these crotchets in groups of 2.

5 Circle these crotchets in groups of 4.

Bars and barlines

When we write music we use a **barline** to group the beats. The area between each line is called a **bar**. A **double barline** shows the end of the music.

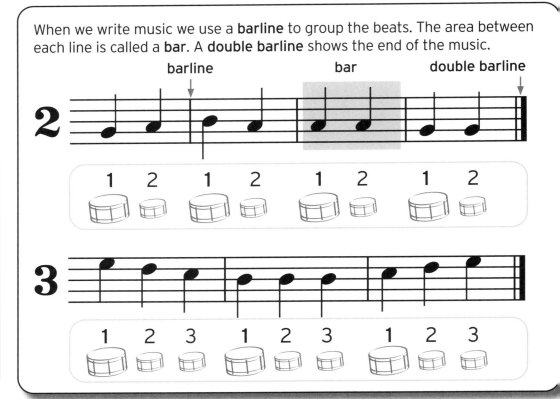

Remember

Make sure your barlines are straight and vertical.

Group these crotchets using barlines. Use a double barline at the end of each exercise.

1

2

3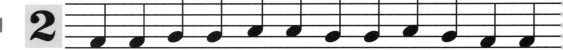

4

Time signatures

There is usually a **time signature** at the beginning of a piece of music.
The top number of the time signature shows the number of beats.
The bottom number shows what type of beats to count (4 means crotchet).

For example, here is a time signature that shows there are 3 crotchet beats in each bar.

| 1 | 2 | 3 | 1 | 2 | 3 | 1 | 2 | 3 |

Copy each time signature five times. Then fill in the boxes.

1    2   in a bar

2   in a bar

3 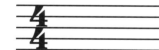   in a bar

Handy tip!

Printed music often contains time signatures that look like this: 2/4

When writing by hand you don't need to shade them.

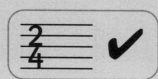

 ✗

 ✗

Time signatures and barlines

1   Write time signatures to agree with the bars.

2   Write the correct number of crotchets on line 2.

3   Write the correct number of crotchets in space 3.

4   Write the correct number of crotchets on line 5.

5   Add bar lines to agree with the time signatures.

Remember

Write a double barline at the end of each exercise.

More time signature practice

Write the correct number of crotchets.
Start on line 2 and go up by step.

Write the correct number of crotchets.
Start in space 3 and stay the same.

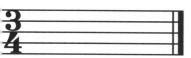

Write the correct number of crotchets.
Start on line 5 and go down by step.

Write the correct number of crotchets.
Start in space 2 and go up by step.

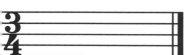

Write the correct number of crotchets.
Start in space 3 and go up by step.

Write the correct number of crotchets.
Start on line 2 and go up by step.

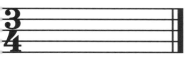

7 Write the correct number of crotchets.
Start on line 5 and stay the same.

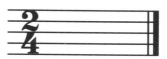

8 Write the correct number of crotchets.
Start on line 3 and go down by step.

9 Write the correct number of crotchets.
Start in space 1 and go up by step.

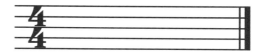

10 Write the correct number of crotchets.
Start in space 4 and go down by step.

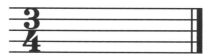

Remember

Count lines and
spaces from the
bottom of the stave.

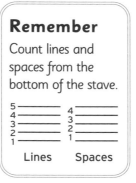

Time signatures (♩ ♪ 𝅗𝅥 o note values)

We know that in music there are short and longer sounds. These are also usually organised within a time signature.

For example, here is a time signature that shows there are 4 crotchet beats in each bar:

1 Write time signatures to agree with the bars.

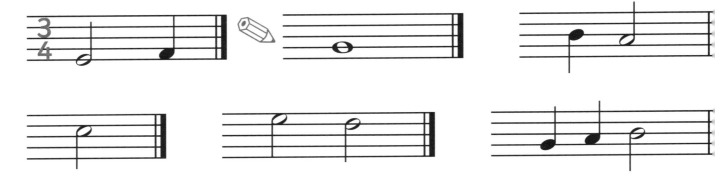

2 Write a minim on line 2. Then use crotchet(s) to complete the bar if necessary.

3 Use notes (♩, 𝅗𝅥 or o) to agree with the time signatures. Write them in space 3.

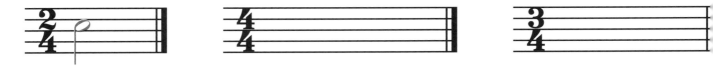

4a Add bar lines to agree with the time signatures.

4b

4c

4d

4e

4f

> **Remember**
> Write a double barline at the end of each exercise.

Writing crotchet rests

Silence is important in music. It gives contrast and shape. In music we call a silence a **rest**.

𝄽 = 1 crotchet beat of silence

Handy tip!
To begin with it is tricky to draw crotchet rests. Think of them in two stages but try to draw them as one continuous line from the top.

Remember
When you draw crotchet rests you don't need to shade them.

𝄽 not 𝄽

1 Draw over these crotchet rests.

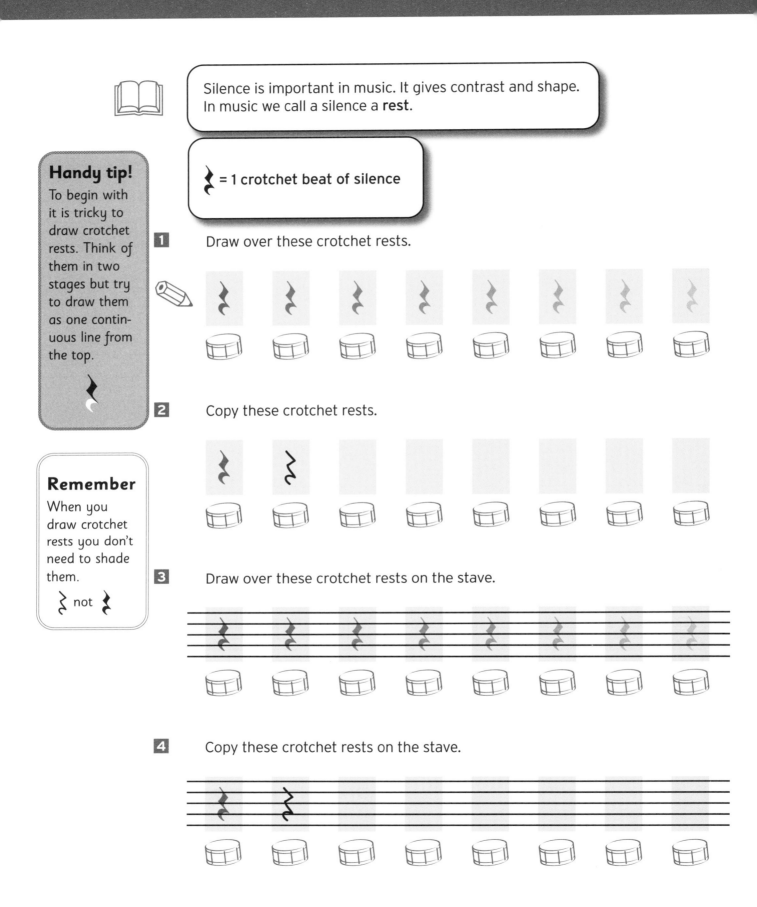

2 Copy these crotchet rests.

3 Draw over these crotchet rests on the stave.

4 Copy these crotchet rests on the stave.

Writing minim rests

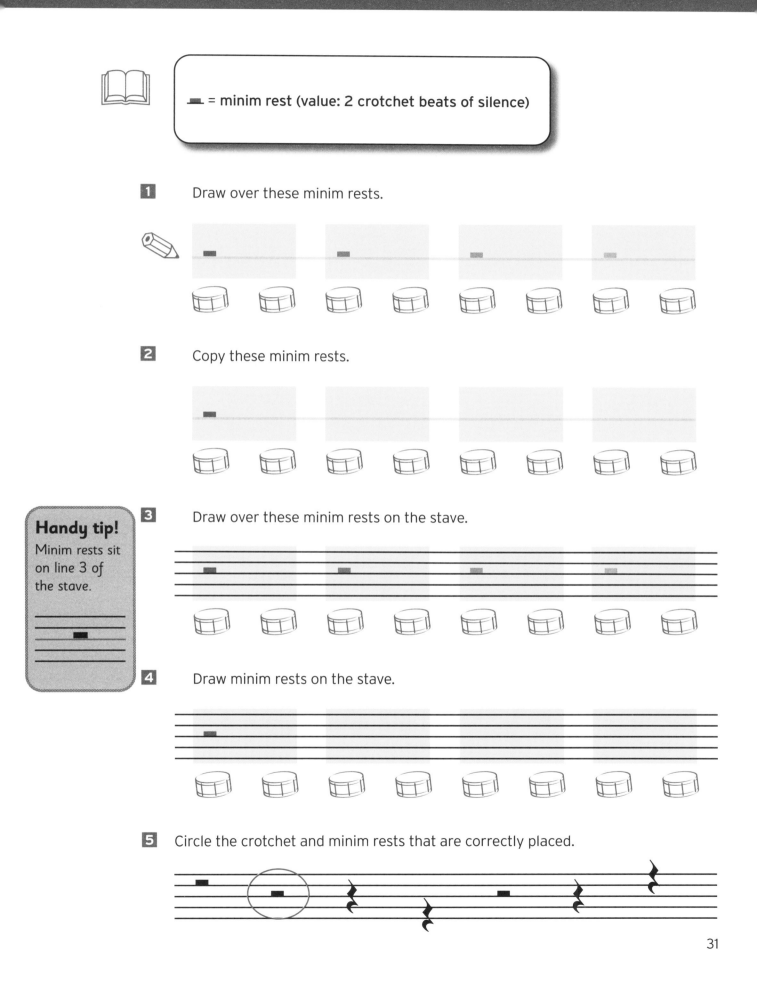

= minim rest (value: 2 crotchet beats of silence)

1 Draw over these minim rests.

2 Copy these minim rests.

Handy tip!
Minim rests sit on line 3 of the stave.

3 Draw over these minim rests on the stave.

4 Draw minim rests on the stave.

5 Circle the crotchet and minim rests that are correctly placed.

Writing semibreve rests

☐ = semibreve rest (value: 4 crotchet beats of silence *or* a whole bar of silence in any time signature)

1 Draw over these semibreve rests.

Handy tip!
Semibreve rests hang from line 4 of the stave.

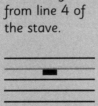

2 Draw over these semibreve rests on the stave.

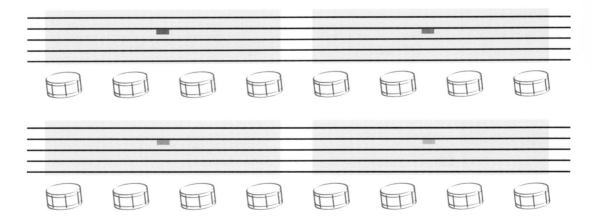

3 Circle the semibreve rests.

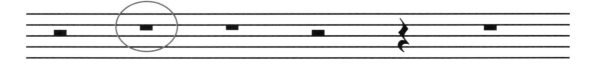

4 Draw semibreve rests on the stave.

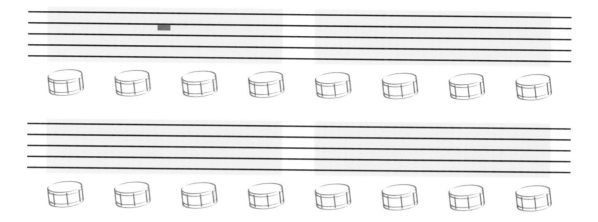

5 Circle the semibreve rests that are correctly drawn.

Adding note and rest values

Add the total number of crotchet beats in these note and rest values.

1

= **4** crotchet beats

2

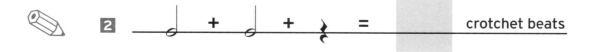

= crotchet beats

3   ♩ + ▬ =   crotchet beats

4   𝄾 + 𝄾 + ▬ =   crotchet beats

5   𝅗𝅥 + 𝄾 + ▬ =   crotchet beats

6   𝅗𝅥 + ▬ =   crotchet beats

7   𝅗𝅥 + 𝅝 + 𝄾 =   crotchet beats

8   𝄾 + ▬ + 𝅝 =   crotchet beats

9   𝅗𝅥 + ▬ =   crotchet beats

10   𝅝 + ♩ =   crotchet beats

Time signatures (using note and rest values)

We know that short and longer sounds in music are usually organised within a time signature. Short or longer silences, or rests, are also organised in this way.

Here are the note and rest values we know organised in the time signature of $\frac{4}{4}$

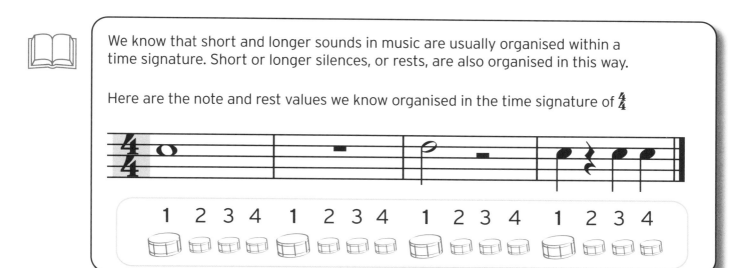

1 Write time signatures to agree with the bars.

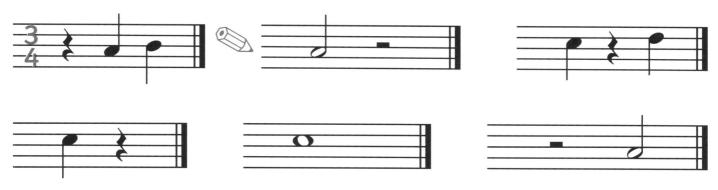

2 Write a minim in space 4. Then use a rest to complete the bar if necessary.

3 Write rests to complete the bars.

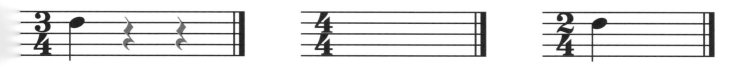

Remember

 = semibreve rest (value: 4 crotchet beats of silence or
a whole bar of silence in any time signature)

4a Add bar lines to agree with the time signatures.

4b

4c

4d

4e

4f

The musical alphabet

Each note is labelled with a letter name from the alphabet, **A B C D E F G**.
It repeats over and over again as the notes get higher.
This is easiest to 'see' on a keyboard because each key is visible. If you have a keyboard, play and sing the note names. If not, ask your teacher to show you.

Look!

The black and white notes form a pattern on the keyboard. This makes each note easy to find.

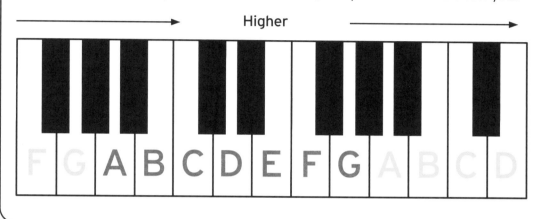

1 Fill in the missing letter names on these keyboard pictures.

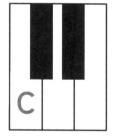  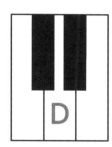 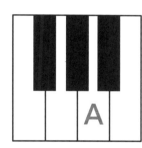

Fill in the missing letters of the musical alphabet.

Handy tip!

As you write each note name sing it in your head, going up by step.

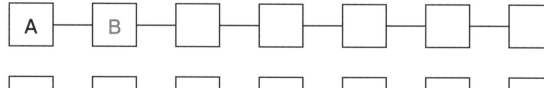

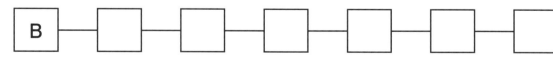

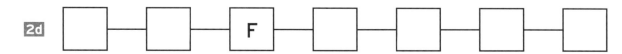

Clefs

You already know that we write music on a 5-line stave. This helps us to show sounds that go up, go down or stay the same.

getting higher   getting lower   staying the same

We usually write a **clef** at the beginning of each stave. It pins a particular note from the musical alphabet to a stave line.

1 Write an arrow pointing to line 2 to show that it is G on this stave.

 2 Write an arrow pointing to line 4 to show that it is F on this stave.

3 Write an arrow pointing to line 2 to show that it is G on this stave.

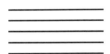

Did you know?

The signs for clefs evolved from letters of the musical alphabet.
The G clef (now called the treble clef) looks a bit like an old-fashioned G

The F clef (now called the bass clef) looks a bit like an old-fashioned F

The treble clef (or G clef)

Did you know?
We usually use capital letters to name notes in the musical alphabet.

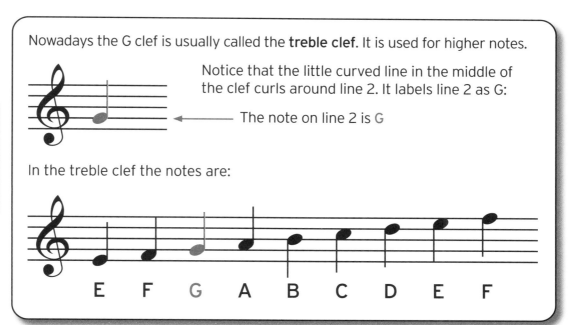

Nowadays the G clef is usually called the **treble clef**. It is used for higher notes.

Notice that the little curved line in the middle of the clef curls around line 2. It labels line 2 as G:

The note on line 2 is G

In the treble clef the notes are:

E F G A B C D E F

1 Write over the dotted lines to make treble clefs. Draw them as one continuous line.

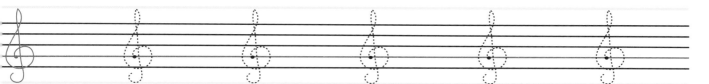

2 Complete these treble clefs.

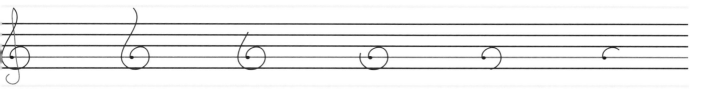

3 Draw a treble clef. Then name the notes using the musical alphabet.

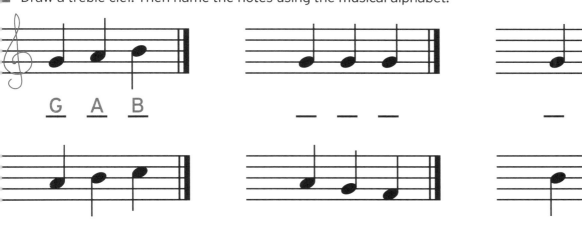

G A B

Treble clef lines and spaces

Not all notes stay the same or move by step. They sometimes skip a note from line to line or space to space, going up or down.

Treble clef lines:

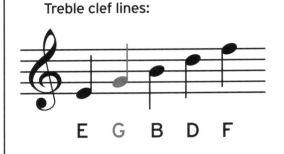

E G B D F

Treble clef spaces:

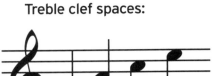

F A C E

Did you know?

People sometimes make up phrases or words to help remember treble-clef lines and spaces, such as:
Every **G**reen **B**us **D**rives **F**ast (lines) and **FACE** (spaces)

---

1 Draw a treble clef. Then name the notes using the musical alphabet.

G   B   _

_ _ _

_ _ _

2

_ _ _

_ _ _

_ _ _

3

_ _ _

_ _ _

_ _ _

Draw a treble clef. Then write crotchets to match the note names.

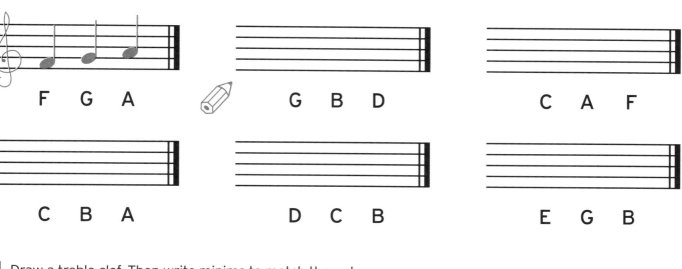

F   G   A   G   B   D   C   A   F

C   B   A   D   C   B   E   G   B

Draw a treble clef. Then write minims to match the note names.

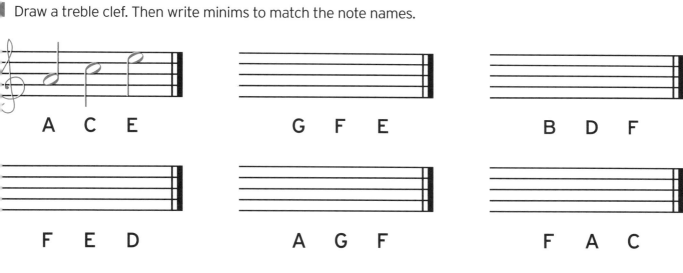

A   C   E   G   F   E   B   D   F

F   E   D   A   G   F   F   A   C

Draw a treble clef. Then write semibreves to match the note names.

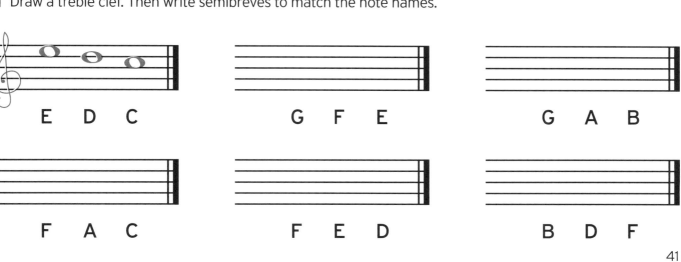

E   D   C   G   F   E   G   A   B

F   A   C   F   E   D   B   D   F

The bass clef (or F clef)

Nowadays the F clef is usually called the **bass clef**. It is used for lower notes.

Notice that the little dots of the clef go on either side of line 4. It labels it as F:

← The note on line 4 is F

In the bass clef the notes are:

G   A   B   C   D   E   F   G   A

1 Write over the dotted lines to make bass clefs

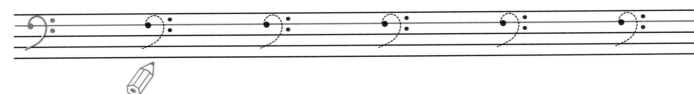

2 Write bass clefs. Check that the dots go on either side of line 4.

3 Draw a bass clef. Then name the notes using the musical alphabet.

> **Notice**
> When notes are going down the musical alphabet names go backwards.

F   E   D

—   —   —

—   —   —

—   —   —

—   —   —

Bass clef lines and spaces

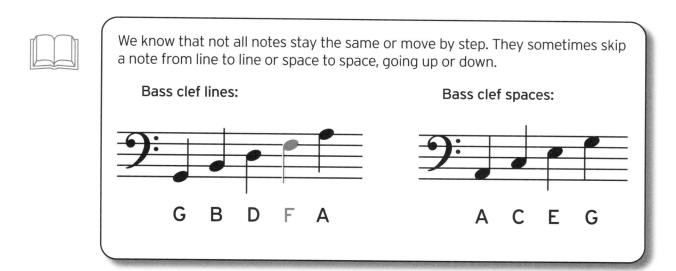

We know that not all notes stay the same or move by step. They sometimes skip a note from line to line or space to space, going up or down.

Bass clef lines:

G   B   D   F   A

Bass clef spaces:

A   C   E   G

Handy tip!

People sometimes make up phrases to help remember lines and spaces.
Can you think of any for the bass clef lines and spaces?

1 Draw a bass clef. Then name the notes using the musical alphabet.

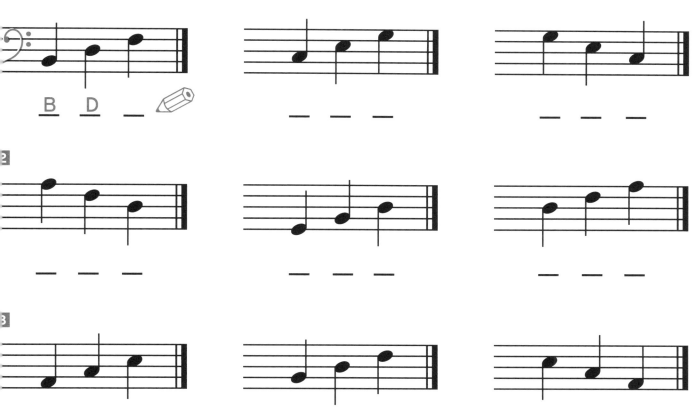

B   D   _

_   _   _

_   _   _

2

_   _   _

_   _   _

_   _   _

3

_   _   _

_   _   _

_   _   _

4 Draw a bass clef. Then write crotchets to match the note names.

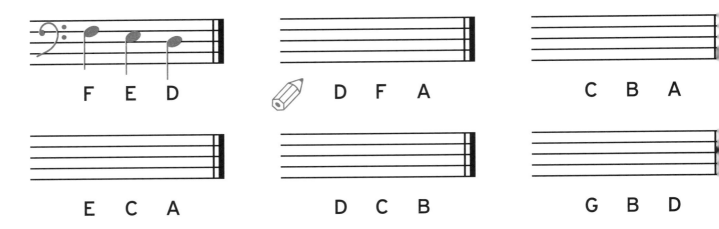

F E D   D F A   C B A

E C A   D C B   G B D

5 Draw a bass clef. Then write minims to match the note names.

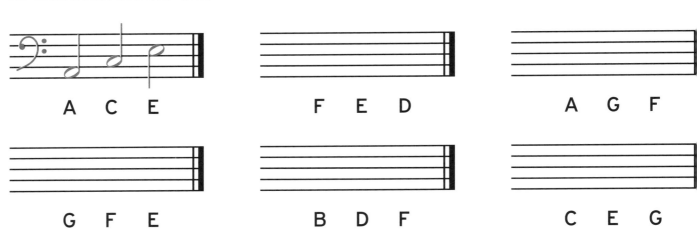

A C E   F E D   A G F

G F E   B D F   C E G

6 Draw a bass clef. Then write semibreves to match the note names.

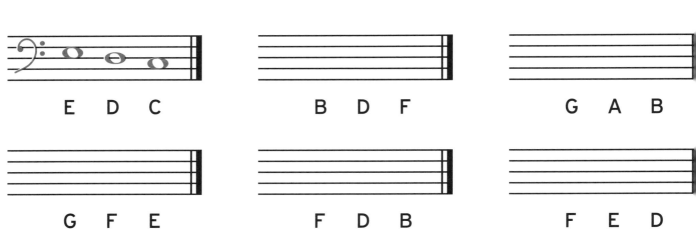

E D C   B D F   G A B

G F E   F D B   F E D

Treble clef and time signature practice

raw a treble clef. Then, where necessary, complete each bar with the named note to agree with the time signature.

Bass clef and time signature practice

Draw a bass clef. Then, where necessary complete each bar with the named note to agree with the time signature

Accidentals – flats, sharps and naturals

Did you know?
Accidentals are signs that we sometimes use to change the pitch of a note.
There are three types — **flats**, **sharps** and **naturals**.
The following pages will set you up well for the Grade 1 workbook, where you will learn what they mean.

Handy tip!
Write flat signs in two parts:

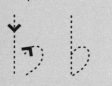

Flats

Here is a **flat sign** on a line and in a space.

The flat sign sits just before the notehead. Notice that it is positioned differently for the note on a line and the note in a space.

Handy tip!
The curved part of your flat sign should look like half a heart, not a b.

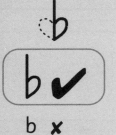

1 Write over the dotted lines to make flat signs.

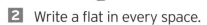

2 Write a flat in every space.

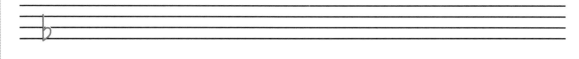

3 Write a flat on every line.

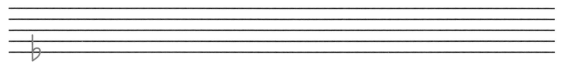

4 Write a flat before each note.

Sharps

Here is a **sharp sign** on a line and in a space.

The sharp sign sits just before the notehead. Notice that it is positioned differently for the note on a line and the note in a space.

Handy tip!
Write the downward lines first:

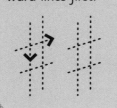

1 Write over the dotted lines to make sharp signs.

Look!
The second set of lines are parallel **and** slanted so that they don't get muddled up with the stave lines.

2 Write a sharp in every space.

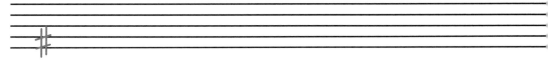

3 Write a sharp on every line.

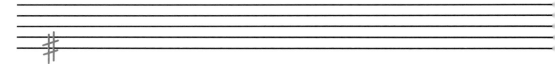

4 Write a sharp before each note.

Handy tip!

48

Naturals

Here is a **natural sign** on a line and in a space.

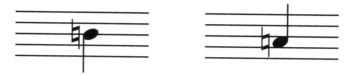

The natural sign sits just before the notehead. Notice that it is positioned differently for the note on a line and the note in a space.

Handy tip!

Write natural signs in two parts:

1 Write over the dotted lines to make natural signs.

2 Write a natural in every space.

3 Write a natural on every line.

4 Write a natural before each note.

Handy tip!

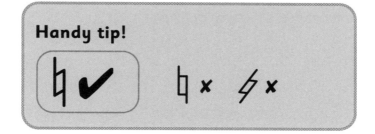

Progress assessment

Section 1

Put a tick (✓) in the box next to the correct answer.

Example

What type of note is this?

Crotchet ☑   Minim ☐   Semibreve ☐

This shows that you think **crotchet** is the correct answe[r]

1.1   What type of note is this?

Semibreve ☐   Crotchet ☐   Minim ☐

1.2   How many crotchet beats are there in a semibreve?

1 ☐   2 ☐   4 ☐

1.3   How many crotchet beats of silence in this rest?

2 ☐   1 ☐   4 ☐

1.4   Which rest matches the length of this note value?

☐   ☐   ☐

1.5   Add the total number of crotchet beats in these note values:

=   2 ☐   3 ☐   4 ☐

1.6   Add the total number of crotchet beats in these rest values:

=   2 ☐   1 ☐   3 ☐

7   Which note is on a line?

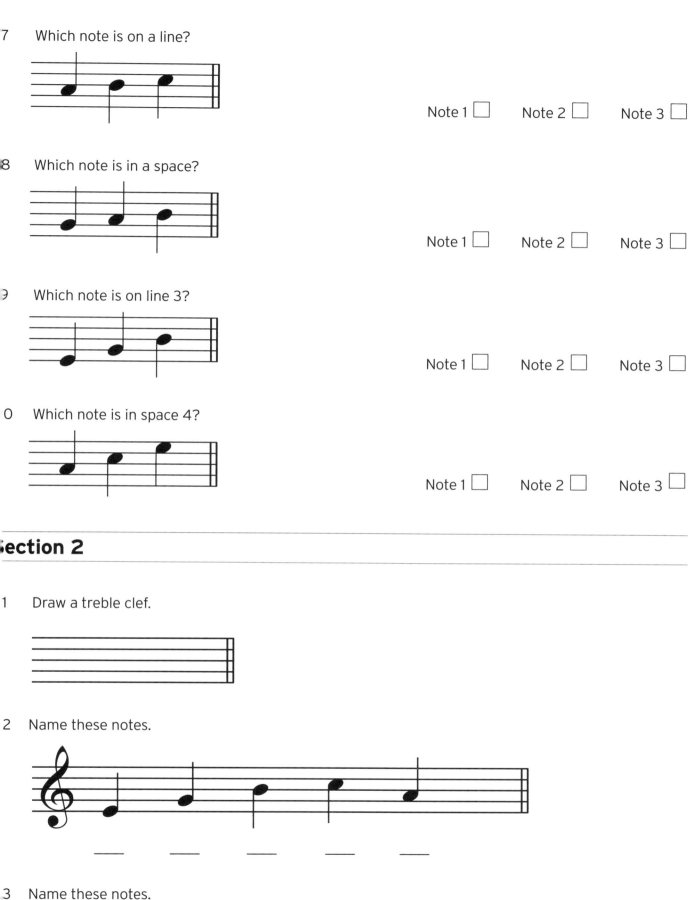

Note 1 ☐   Note 2 ☐   Note 3 ☐

8   Which note is in a space?

Note 1 ☐   Note 2 ☐   Note 3 ☐

9   Which note is on line 3?

Note 1 ☐   Note 2 ☐   Note 3 ☐

0   Which note is in space 4?

Note 1 ☐   Note 2 ☐   Note 3 ☐

Section 2

1   Draw a treble clef.

2   Name these notes.

___   ___   ___   ___   ___

3   Name these notes.

___   ___   ___   ___   ___

Section 3

3.1   Circle five different mistakes in the following music.

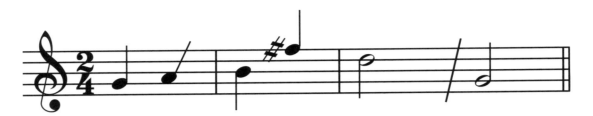

Section 4

4.1   Add barlines to agree with the time signature.

Section 5

5.1   Complete the bars with crotchets.

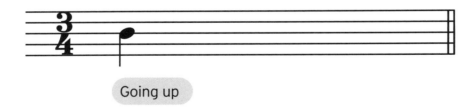

Going up

5.2

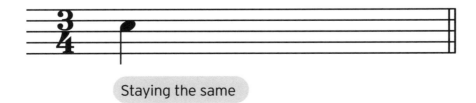

Staying the same

ook at the following music and answer the questions below.

| | Bar 1 | Bar 2 | Bar 3 | Bar 4 |

1   Name the clef. _____

2   How many crotchet beats does the time signature show?_____

3   In which bar is there a note which lasts for four crotchet beats? _____

4   For how many crotchet beats does the rest last in bar 3? _____

5   In which bar are the highest notes in this music? _____

6   In which bar are there crotchets going down? _____

7   In which bar is the lowest note in this music?_____

8   In which bar are there notes that sound the same? _____

9   In which bar is there a rest?_____

10   Why are there two barlines at the end of the music? _____

Writing your own music

Here are some staves for you to write your own music.

Or you might like to use them for extra writing practice, or to copy out a piece.

Different words – same meaning

In music there are often different words to describe the same thing. Try to remember the words below so that you are well prepared for the Grade 1 book.

The American names for note values are included as they are often used and you can use them in future exams if you wish to do so.

bar – measure

bass clef – F clef

beat – pulse, count

crotchet – quarter note

doh – home note, tonic

going down – getting lower

going up – getting higher

minim – half note

pitch – sound, note

semibreve – whole note

stave – staff

treble clef – G clef

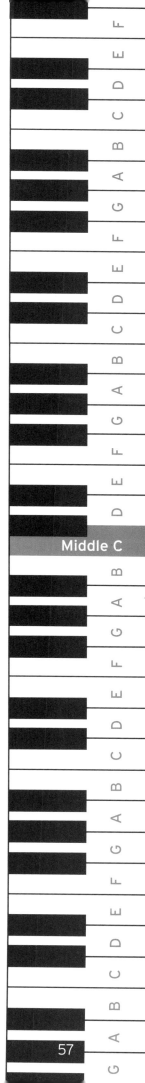

Introducing Theory of Music

First writing skills for musicians

This book has been designed to help the beginner student to read and write commonly used musical symbols, providing a firm grounding in notation from which to progress onto Trinity's Theory of Music Workbook Grade 1.

There is ample opportunity to practise each element throughout this workbook, with symbols often explored in more than one way to build deeper understanding and to consolidate the learning.

'Did you know?', 'Handy tip' and 'Remember' boxes give advice along the way, encouraging the development of good musical handwriting habits. After completing the exercises in this book, any student is sure to feel confident when they begin studying for their first Theory of Music exam.

By Naomi Yandell, author of Trinity's popular Theory of Music Workbook series.

The following Trinity publications are available from **trinitycollege.com/shop** or your local music shop:

Theory of Music Workbook Grade 1	TG 006509	ISBN 978-0-85736-000-7
Aural Tests book 1 (Initial–Grade 5) from 2017	TCL 015808	ISBN 978-0-85736-535-4
Student Practice Notebook	TCL 015310	ISBN 978-0-85736-487-6

All syllabuses and further information about Trinity College London exams can be obtained from trinitycollege.com

TCL 024107
ISBN 978-1-80051-473-7

TRINITY
COLLEGE LONDON PRESS

MINISTRY OF DEFENCE

ministry of defence

Annual Report & Accounts

2003 - 2004